> ERASING THE STIGMA OF
> MENTAL HEALTH ISSUES
> THROUGH AWARENESS

Managing Moods Workbook

A TOOLBOX of REPRODUCIBLE ASSESSMENTS and ACTIVITIES

Ester R. A. Leutenberg
and John J. Liptak, EdD

Stress & Wellness Publishers

Duluth, Minnesota

Whole Person
101 W. 2nd St., Suite 203
Duluth, MN 55802

800-247-6789

books@wholeperson.com
www.wholeperson.com

Managing Moods Workbook
A Toolbox of Reproducible Assessments and Activities

Copyright ©2014 by Ester R.A. Leutenberg and John J. Liptak.
All rights reserved. Except for short excerpts for review purposes and materials in the assessment, journaling activities, and educational handouts sections, no part of this book may be reproduced or transmitted in any form by any means, electronic or mechanical without permission in writing from the publisher. Self-assessments, exercises, and educational handouts are meant to be photocopied.

All efforts have been made to ensure accuracy of the information contained in this book as of the date published. The author(s) and the publisher expressly disclaim responsibility for any adverse effects arising from the use or application of the information contained herein.-

Printed in the United States of America

10 9 8 7 6 5 4 3 2 1

Editorial Director: Carlene Sippola
Art Director: Joy Morgan Dey

Library of Congress Control Number: 2014909594
ISBN: 978-1-57025-319-5

Introduction

Using the *Managing Moods Workbook*

People become sad for a variety of reasons including disappointment, grief, frustration of not being able to accomplish a project or not getting what's desired, experiencing despair during holiday seasons, etc. When these feelings of sadness and/or dysphoric moods last for hours and even days, they may not be a cause for concern. These feelings are part of the normal "ups" and "downs" of life. It is common for people to feel blue or down, become frustrated and/or experience a sense of emptiness from time to time.

However, a sad mood which won't let up can change the way people think and feel and may be a sign of a more serious mood problem. When people find themselves for several weeks taking little joy in activities they have previously enjoyed, appear irritable a majority of the time, and feel fatigue and a general loss of energy, they may be experiencing the symptoms of more serious problems.

These more serious mood problems stretch far beyond the normal limits of disappointment, loss, frustration, and joylessness. Mood problems can be accompanied by an inability to cope with everyday life issues and stressors. Rather than temporary feelings of down in the dumps, these extreme feelings tend to last for more than a few hours or days. These feelings tend to affect all aspects of a person's life and leave the person feeling empty, unable to move, and hopeless for weeks, months and even years.

People who experience problems in maintaining a balanced and healthy overall mood are often incapable of functioning well in daily life. They often experience extreme emotional states, negative feelings, and self-defeating moods that are inconsistent with what is happening in their environment. People struggling with this mental condition find that they are unable to conquer their moodiness in the workplace, at home, with family and friends, at school, and in their community. People who experience moodiness have problems in interpersonal relationships, ability to work effectively, study and concentrate, and in the ways they eat, sleep, relax and live their daily lives.

Our goal for this book is NOT to diagnose a mental illness, or even for the facilitator to make that diagnosis from this book's content. Our goal is to touch on some of the symptoms and possibilities, create realizations, and provide coping methods which will help people to go forward and perhaps consider the possibility of the need for consideration of medications and therapy. It is also to help participants recognize that other people have the same issues, that no shame is connected to them, and mental health issues of any degree is not to be stigmatized nor should anyone need to feel like a victim to stereotyping. In this book, we are using the phrase mental health issues in order to include ALL types of mood problems, from just being moody to serious mental illness.

Our thanks to these professionals who make us look good!
Art Director - Joy Dey
Editor and Lifelong Teacher - Eileen Regen
Editorial Director - Carlene Sippola
Proofreader - Jay Leutenberg
Reviewer - Carol Butler
**Our thanks for helping us launch our new series of serious,
vitally important, yet delicate topics!**
Mel Gallen, Ph.D. and Dr. Raymond K. Lederman

Managing Moods Workbook Can Help Everyone Who is Moody

People experience many different problems related to mood. The assessments and activities in this workbook are designed to provide facilitators with a wide variety of tools to use in helping people manage their moods. Many choices for self-exploration are provided for facilitators to determine which tools best suit the unique needs of their participants.

The purpose of this workbook is to provide a user-friendly guide to short-term assessments and activities designed to help people conquer feelings of moodiness and experience a greater sense of wellbeing. In addition, this workbook is designed to help provide facilitators and participants with tools and information needed to overcome the stigma attached to mood conditions.

In order to help their participants successfully deal with moodiness, it is extremely helpful for facilitators to have a variety of appealing, user-friendly assessments and activities to help their participants "open-up" and begin to feel as if their mood is less intense and more balanced, and that they are not alone. The Managing Moods Workbook provides assessments and self-guided activities to help participants reduce the intensity of moodiness and begin living more effectively.

When to Worry?

Disturbances in mood are much more painful and numbing than the everyday blues and sadness that most people experience. These disturbances are much more than a temporary feeling of being down in the dumps, disappointed, sad after a loss, irritable, angry or frustrated. Ongoing, constant moodiness is a pervasive sense of emptiness in which people are unable to engage with daily life, feel lethargic about everyone and everything, experience a series of both highs and lows, and an immobilization in which getting out of bed can feel like a difficult task. The good news is that people can develop the cognitive, affective, and behavioral skills needed to decrease the amount, depth and duration of their moodiness and begin to feel a sense of joy, contentment, and wellbeing. People who experience these feelings over time are at risk of having a serious mood disturbance and need to seek professional medical and psychological assistance.

Suicide Warning!

People who experience severe bouts of moodiness are often at risk for suicide. Sometimes their feelings can be so strong that they think the only way to escape the pain is to die by suicide. Remember to take any talk about suicide or suicidal acts very seriously. Anyone showing any of the following symptoms needs to be taken seriously, and facilitators can take an active role in their finding help immediately:

- Withdrawing from family, friends, and activities of interest in the past
- Increasing use of harmful substances
- Giving away possessions
- Expressing severe hopelessness about the future
- Making a plan for dying by suicide
- Calling or visiting people to say goodbye
- Getting legal affairs in order
- Engaging in reckless behavior
- Talking about killing or harming self
- Expressing feeling trapped with no way out
- Purchasing a weapon

People need to do much more than complete the assessments, activities and exercises contained in this workbook if they have a serious mental illness. All mood disturbances need to be thoroughly evaluated by a medical professional, and then treated with an appropriate combination of medication and group and/or individual therapy.

Types of Serious Mood Inconsistencies for the Facilitator

Many different types of mood disturbances are conveyed and expressed in different forms. Some of the types of mood disturbances that people typically experience include the following:

Major Depression (often referred to as unipolar depression) involves a profoundly sad mood and a high probability of distorted depressive thinking that occur over time.

Some of the additional symptoms:
- A persistent, sad mood most of the day accompanied by feeling empty
- Experiencing a significant reduction in appetite and weight loss when not dieting, or increased appetite and weight gain
- Sleeping too much (hypersomnia) or an inability to sleep (insomnia)
- Feelings of inadequacy
- Racing thoughts and impulsive behaviors
- Hostility or aggression
- Feelings of agitation or feelings of restlessness
- Fatigue, loss of energy or feelings of being slowed down
- Feelings of worthlessness and hopelessness or excessive or inappropriate guilt
- Diminished ability to think or concentrate, remember things or be decisive
- Constant feelings of anxiety or feelings of irritability
- Loss of interest in activities, or a decrease in pleasure in activities once enjoyed
- Physical symptoms such as headaches, pain, digestive problems
- Thoughts of suicide and/or danger to others

Bipolar Depression involves an alteration (like a roller-coaster ride) of down feelings (depression) and up feelings (excessive and often inappropriate euphoric), rapid speech and hyperactivity.

Some additional symptoms:
- Cycles of elation and depression
- Distinct period of abnormally and persistently elevated and euphoric mood
- Inflated self-esteem or grandiosity
- Decrease in the need for sleep
- Flight of ideas
- Distractibility
- Increased engagement in risky behavior

Milder Forms of Depression carry detectable symptoms and impact daily activities in ways that demonstrate a diminished interest in things people usually find interesting or enjoyable.

Some of these types of mood disturbances:
- Dysthymia – Person has a mild depression that lingers for more than two years. For people with dysthymia, life has little pleasure and they tend to be cranky, irritable, and testy.
- Postpartum Depression – Person experiences depression after childbirth. Sometimes called *baby blues*, this type of depression may be associated with psychological and physical factors.
- Seasonal Affective Disorder – Person experiences depression with seasonal changes in climate and light.

Depression From Unknown Origin includes feelings of sadness and emptiness, low energy, and a lack of interest that occurs naturally when experiencing change or stress in life. Unlike the feelings of sadness and moodiness that are part of everyday life, many people are often unable to deal with their feelings of sadness and moodiness and their feelings last much longer. The mood is accompanied by feelings of irritability and hostility, a growing sense of fatigue, and a sense of hopelessness about the future.

Sources of Serious Mood Inconsistencies

Where do disturbances in mood originate? Why do some people experience changes in mood and moodiness, while others do not? That is not an easy question to answer. Because mood inconsistencies are very complex in nature, they usually do not originate from one source. Rather, many things can lead to mood disturbances in people, and often it is not one of the following sources, but a combination of several sources.

Negative Thinking

Distorted, maladaptive, and irrational thinking can cause and enhance feelings of sadness and moodiness. A thorough examination should be conducted of a participant's thought processes as they relate to and affect feelings.

Genetics and Biology

Family history can influence one's predisposition to moodiness. A complete medical and psychological history should be completed to identify family members who may also have experienced periods of sadness.

Uncontrollable Situations

Situations in which people find themselves unable to control the outcomes can enhance feelings of sadness, a loss of interest, and a sense of hopelessness and helplessness. An examination of the situations in which participants experience feelings of moodiness should be conducted by a medical/psychological professional.

Life Events

An inability to cope with major stressors can be a factor in moodiness. Some of the major stressors that often precede mood disturbances include separation and divorce, traumatic shock, legal troubles, feeling stuck in a situation without an exit, loss of a loved one, and loss of a job. An examination of the life events that may be causing sadness and moodiness should be conducted by a medical/psychological professional.

Medical Conditions

People who have medical conditions often experience mood disturbances as a secondary symptom. A participant's medical history can reveal conditions that might induce a mood problem and should be examined by a medical/psychological professional.

Substances

People often experience mood problems from chronic use of alcohol and drugs. An examination of a participant's drug and alcohol abuse should be examined by a medical/psychological professional.

Lack of Social Support

People who have access to a social support system are much less likely to experience severe and extended bouts of sadness. An examination of participant's support system should be conducted by a medical/psychological professional.

Format of the Managing Moods Workbook

The *Managing Moods Workbook* is designed to be used either independently or as part of an established mental health issue program. You may administer any of the assessments and the guided self-exploration activities to an individual or a group with whom you are working, and you may administer any of the assessments and activities over one or more days. Feel free to pick and choose those that best fit the outcomes you desire. The purpose of this workbook is to provide facilitators who work with individuals and groups who may be experiencing mood disturbances with a series of reproducible activities that can be used to supplement their work with participants. Because the activity pages in this workbook are reproducible, they can be photocopied as is, or changes made with white out, or adding additional words to a master, to suit each group, and then photocopied.

Assessments

Assessments (scales for each individual mode) establish a behavioral baseline from which facilitators and participants can gauge progress toward identified goals. This workbook will supplement a facilitator's work by providing assessments designed to measure behavioral baselines for measuring client change. In order to do so, assessments with scoring directions and interpretation materials begin each module. The authors recommend that you begin presenting each topic by asking participants to complete the assessment. Facilitators can choose one or more, or all of the activities relevant to their participants' specific needs and concerns.

Each of the awareness modules contained in this book begin with an assessment for these purposes:
- Help facilitators to develop a numerical baseline of behavior, attitude, and personality characteristics before they begin their plan of treatment.
- Help facilitators gather valuable information about themselves.
- Help facilitators in the measurement of change over time.
- Use assessments as pre-tests and post-tests to measure changes in behavior, attitude, and personality.
- Use assessments to help facilitators identify patterns that are negatively affecting a participant.
- Prompt insight and behavioral change.
- Help participants feel part of the treatment-planning process.
- Provide participants with a starting point to begin to learn more about themselves and their strengths and limitations.

Assessments are a great aid in developing plans for effective change and decreased moodiness. Be aware of the following when administering, scoring and interpreting assessments in this workbook:
- The purpose of these assessments is not to pigeonhole people, but to allow them to explore various elements of themselves and their situations.
- This book contains self-assessments and not tests. Traditional tests measure knowledge or right or wrong responses. For the assessments provided in this book, remind participants that there are no right or wrong answers. These assessments ask only for opinions or attitudes.
- The assessments in this workbook have face value, but have not been formally normed for validity and reliability.
- The assessments in this workbook are based on self-reported data. In other words, the accuracy and usefulness of the information is dependent on the information that participants honestly provide about themselves. Assure them that they do not need to share their information. They can be honest.
- The assessments are exploratory exercises and not a judgment of who they are as human beings.
- The assessments are not a substitute for professional assistance. If you feel any of your participants need more assistance than you can provide, refer them to an appropriate professional.

Format of the *Managing Moods Workbook*

Assessment Script

When administering the assessments contained in this workbook, please remember that the assessments can be administered, scored, and interpreted by the client. If working in a group, facilitators should circulate among participants as they complete assessments to ensure that there are no questions. If working with an individual client, facilitators can use the instruction collaboratively. **Please note that as your participants begin the assessments in this workbook, the instructions below are meant to be a guide, so please do not feel you must say them word for word.**

Tell your participants: *"You will be completing a quick assessment related to the topics we are discussing. Assessments are powerful tools, but only if you are honest with yourself. Take your time and be truthful in your responses so that your results are an honest reflection of you. Your level of commitment in completing the assessments honestly will determine how much you learn about yourself. You do not need to share them with anyone if you don't want to."*

Allow participants to turn to the first page of their assessment and read the instructions silently to themselves, then tell them: *"All of the assessments have similar formats, but they have different scales, responses, scoring instructions and methods for interpretation. If you do not understand how to complete the assessment, ask me before you turn the page to begin."*

Then tell them: *"Because there is no time limit for completing the assessments, take your time and work at your own pace. Do not answer the assessments as you think others would like you to answer them or how you think others see you. These assessments are for you to reflect on your life and explore some of the barriers that are keeping you from living a more satisfying life. Before completing each assessment, be sure to read the instructions."*

Make sure that nobody has a question, then tell them: *"Learning about yourself can be a positive and motivating experience. Don't stress about taking the assessments or discovering your results. Just respond honestly and learn as much about yourself as you can."*

Tell participants to turn the page and begin answering with Question 1. Allow sufficient time for all participants to complete their assessment. Answer any questions people have. It is extremely helpful for you, as the facilitator, to read and/or complete the assessment prior to distributing to the participants. As people begin to finish, read through the instructions for scoring the assessment. Have participants begin to score their assessments and transfer their scores for interpretation being sure that no one has a question about the scoring.

Review the purpose of the interpretation table included after each assessment. Tell the participants: *"Remember, this assessment was not designed to label you. Rather, it was designed to develop a baseline of your behaviors. Regardless of how you score on an assessment, consider it a starting point upon which you can develop healthier habits. Take your time, reflect on your results, and note how they compare to what you already know about yourself."*

After participants have completed, scored, and interpreted their assessment, facilitators can use the self-exploration activities included in each module to supplement their traditional tools and techniques to help participants function more effectively.

(Continued on the next page)

Format of the *Managing Moods Workbook* (Continued)

Self-Exploration Activities

This workbook will provide self-exploration activities that can be used to induce behavioral change, enhance thinking skills and decrease feelings of sadness and moodiness. These activities, included after each of the assessments, will prompt self-reflection and promote self-understanding. They use a variety of formats to accommodate all learning styles and foster introspection and promote pro-social behaviors, life skills and coping skills. The activities in each section correlate to the assessments to enable you to identify and select activities quickly and easily.

Self-exploration activities assist participants in self-reflection, enhance self-knowledge, identify potential ineffective behaviors, and teach more effective ways of coping with moodiness. They are designed to help participants make a series of discoveries that lead to increased social and emotional competencies, as well as to serve as an energizing way to help participants grow personally and professionally. These brief, easy-to-use self-reflection tools are designed to promote insight and self-growth.

Many different types of guided self-exploration activities are provided for you to pick and choose the activities that are most needed by your participants and the ones that will be most appealing to them. The unique features of the exploration activities make them user-friendly and appropriate for a variety of individual sessions and group sessions.

In some activities, participants will have an opportunity to …

- explore how they could make changes in their lives to feel better. These activities are designed to help participants reflect on their current life situations, discover new ways of living more effectively, and implement changes in their lives to accommodate these skills.
- to journal as a way of enhancing their self-awareness. Through journaling prompts, participants will be able to write about the thoughts, attitudes, feelings, and behaviors that have contributed to, or are currently contributing to, their current life situation. Through journaling, participants are able to safely address their concerns, hopes and dreams for the future.
- to explore their moodiness issues by examining past behavior for negative patterns and learning new ways of dealing more effectively in the future. These activities are designed to help participants reflect on their lives in ways that will allow them to develop healthier lifestyles.

The facilitator has the choice of how to process the activities – individually, as a group, volunteers sharing, etc.

The Stigma Awareness Approach

It is important that facilitators keep an open mind about mental health issues and the stigma attached to people experiencing these issues. Rather than thinking of people as having a mental disorder, or being mentally ill, the *Erasing the Stigma of Mental Health Issues through Awareness* series is designed to help facilitators to diminish the stigma that surrounds people suffering from moodiness. Stigmas occur when people are unduly labeled, which sets the stage for discrimination and humiliation. Facilitators are able to help to erase the stigma of mental illness through enhanced awareness of the factors that activate the issues, accentuate the depth of the problems, and accelerate awareness and understanding.

To assist you, a module entitled *Erasing the Stigma of Mental Health Issues* is included to provide activities for helping to erase the stigma associated with mood inconsistencies.

The Awareness Modules

The reproducible awareness modules in this workbook will help you identify and select assessments and activities easily and quickly:

Module I: How Moody Are You?

This module will help participants identify the depth of their moodiness and identify ways to decrease the intensity of this moodiness.

Module II: Effects of Moodiness

This module will help participants identify the ways that moodiness is affecting their health, relationships, work and social activities.

Module III: Mood Triggers

This module will help participants identify the ways that they experience moodiness in their lives through feelings, thoughts, and behaviors.

Module IV: Roller Coaster Moods

This module will help participants identify the effects of mood instabilities in their lives.

Module V: Erasing the Stigma of Mental Health Issues

This module will help participants explore the stigma of moodiness in their lives and the impact that the stigma has on them.

Table of Contents

Module I – How Moody Are You? 15

How Moody Are You? Introduction and Directions 17
How Moody Are You? Scale. 18
Scoring Directions 19
Profile Interpretation 19
Thinking About Your Own Thinking 20
Converting Negative to Positive Thinking 21
Lifestyle Changes 22
Reducing Stress 23
External Causes of Moodiness 24–25
When My Life Was Better 26–27
My Feelings 28–29
Building Resilience 30
Hiding and Mirroring Emotions 31
Just Do It! 32
Feeling Moody 33
A Letter to Me 34
To Understand Me. 35

Module II – Effects of Moodiness 37

Effects of Moodiness Introduction and Directions 39
Effects of Moodiness Scale 40–41
Scoring Directions 42
Profile Interpretation 42
Individual Scale Descriptions 42
My Personal Health 43
Managing My Moodiness 44–45
Let's Get Physical 46
Relationships 47
The Impact on My Relationships 48
Involving Family and Friends 49
Moodiness at Work 50
Managing My Moodiness at Work 51
Social Activities 52
Get Involved Socially 53
Activating Events 54
Reverse Your Negative Thinking 55
Positive Activity Schedule 56
I Have Choices 57

Table of Contents

Module III – Mood Triggers 59

Mood Triggers Scale Introduction and Directions 61
Mood Triggers Scale 62–63
Scoring Directions 64
Profile Interpretation 64
Scale Descriptions 64
My Mood Pattern 65
My Treatment History 66
Early Warning Signs 67–68
I'm Overwhelmed 69
Exercise 70
You Are What You Eat 71
Relaxation Techniques 72
That's Funny 73
When I'm Getting Worse 74
My Internal Triggers 75
Victim Thinking 76
Worry, Worry, Worry 77
My Self-Esteem 78–79

Module IV – Roller Coaster Moods 81

Roller Coaster Moods Scale Introduction and Directions 83
Roller Coaster Moods Scale 84
Scoring Directions 85
Profile Interpretation 85
Over Excited? Frantic? Frenzied? Agitated? 86
Early Warning Signs 87–88
Major Life Decisions 89
To Take or Not To Take? 90
Street Drugs and Alcohol 91
Outlets for Excessive Energy 92
Damage-Repair 93
My WEEKLY Mood Chart 94
My DAILY Mood Chart 95
Potential Support Network 96
My Impulsive Up-Side Behaviors 97
My Social Rhythms 98
Activity vs Inactivity 99
Predictable and Unpredictable Changes 100
Listening 101

Table of Contents

Module V – Erasing the Stigma of Mental Health Issues ...103

    Erasing the Stigma of Mental Health Issues Introduction 105
    Two Types of Mental Health Stigma.........................106
    The Stigma of Being Known as "Moody" – THE PAST..............107
    The Stigma of Being Known as "Moody" – THE FUTURE.............108
    What Animal are YOU? 109
    If we stamp out the stigma... 110
    My Trusted Social Network................................111
    Glenn Close said... 112
    Effects of the Stigma of Moodiness 113
    Stereotypes..114
    Coping with the Stigma of Moodiness 115
    What Can YOU Do?....................................116
    Focus on Your Strengths 117
    My Negative Thoughts...................................118
    Ways I Try to Minimize My Moodiness 119
    Ways I am Treated 120
    Stay Active 121
    Self-Doubt 122
    A Poster About the Stigma of Moodiness 123
    DE-STIGMA-TIZE with the Facts 124

MODULE I

How Moody Are You?

Nothing lifts me out of a bad mood better than a hard workout on my treadmill. It never fails. To us, exercise is nothing short of a miracle.

~ *Cher*

Name _____

Date _____

Managing Moods

How Moody Are You? Scale Introduction and Directions

All people get moody from time to time, but when your moodiness becomes debilitating and begins to interfere with your effectiveness and your relationships in daily life, you need to explore how moody you really are.

You can use the following scale to explore how moody you are in your daily life.

There is a wide range of emotions within moodiness. This assessment contains 25 statements related to your level of moodiness. Read each of the statements and decide how much the statement describes you.

- If the statement describes you a lot, circle the number under that column next to that item.
- If the statement describes you sometimes, circle the number under that column next to that item.
- If the statement describes you only a little or not at all, circle the number under that column next to that item.

In the following example, the circled number under "A Lot" indicates the statement is descriptive of the person completing the inventory a lot of the time.

	A LOT	SOMETIMES	LITTLE/NONE
I have sleep difficulty — either I have trouble sleeping or I sleep too much	(3)	2	1

This is not a test. Since there are no right or wrong answers, do not spend too much time thinking about your answers. Be sure to respond to every statement.

Turn to the next page and begin.

Managing Moods

How Moody Are You? Scale

	A LOT	SOMETIMES	LITTLE/NONE
I have sleep difficulty – either I have trouble sleeping or I sleep too much	3	2	1
I have quick swings in mood from glad to sad	3	2	1
I have appetite problems – either I have no appetite or I can't stop eating	3	2	1
I am irritable around others	3	2	1
I am more aggressive than usual	3	2	1
I feel fatigued and sluggish	3	2	1
I do not share information about my moodiness with family	3	2	1
I tend to be negative most of the time	3	2	1
I have lost my inner peace and contentment	3	2	1
I engage in reckless behavior (driving, substances, etc.)	3	2	1
I don't want people to know that I have a mood problems	3	2	1
I have lost interest in my usual daily activities	3	2	1
I feel *empty*	3	2	1
I do not discuss my moodiness with friends	3	2	1
I feel as if my life is hopeless	3	2	1
I think about suicide	3	2	1
I am critical of myself	3	2	1
I feel embarrassed after I am moody	3	2	1
I have trouble controlling my temper	3	2	1
I have lost interest in sexual activity	3	2	1
I cry	3	2	1
I feel restless	3	2	1
I find it hard to concentrate	3	2	1
I can't seem to "get going"	3	2	1
Even if asked, I will not talk to people about my moods	3	2	1

TOTAL = _____

How Moody Are You? Scale
Scoring Directions

Moodiness can interfere with your relationships, work, school, social activities, and participation in the community. The How Moody Are You? Scale is designed to help you explore how persistent your feelings of moodiness are and how disruptive your moods are in your daily life.

For the scale you just completed, add the numbers that you circled. This score will give you some sense of how moody you are. Your total will range from 25 to 75.

Then, transfer this total to the space below:

Level of Moodiness Total   =   _____

Profile Interpretation

Individual Scale Score	Result	Indications
25 to 41	Low	Low scores indicate a low level of moodiness. Complete the following exercises to ensure you reduce your moody feelings even further.
42 to 58	Moderate	Moderate scores indicate a medium high level of moodiness. Complete the following exercises to ensure you reduce your moody feelings even further.
59 to 75	High	High scores indicate a high level of moodiness. Complete the following exercises to ensure you reduce your moody feelings even further.

WARNING

People who are experiencing moderate and high levels of moody feelings, thoughts and behaviors can be at risk for suicide. Sometimes moody feelings can be so strong that people think that the only way to escape the pain is to attempt suicide. You need to remember that if you are having these feelings, or spend time thinking about how you could take your life, you need to talk to a medical professional. The following activities are designed to help reduce your level of moodiness. Regardless of how you scored on the scale, please complete all of the activities.

Managing Moods

Thinking About Your Own Thinking

People who experience mood disturbances often engage in negative thinking. There are many different methods of negative thinking. Which ones describe your thinking?

Type of Negative Thinking	My Negative Thoughts	How They Make Me Feel and Act
Self-Doubt (Example: I'm not good enough, I'm too fat, etc.)		
Pessimism (Example: I'm doomed, Nothing ever works out, etc.)		
Powerlessness (Example: I can't help myself, etc.)		
Demanding Thinking (Example: I should have, I must, etc.)		
Negativism (Example: Focusing on the negative in a situation)		

Which type of thinking do you exhibit most often? How can you be more alert to this type of thinking? _____

_____

Converting Negative to Positive Thinking

You can work to translate your negative thinking into more positive thinking. Complete the table below based on the negative thoughts you identified.

My Negative Thoughts	More Accurate Positive Thoughts	My Affirmation
Example: "I'll never be good enough."	"I don't need to compare myself to others."	"I am good enough just as I am."

Managing Moods

Lifestyle Changes

Lifestyle changes are those small changes that you can make for yourself to feel better and be less moody. Lifestyle changes can encompass many different aspects of your life.

Complete the table below to explore lifestyle changes you could make.

Aspects of My Lifestyle	Current Lifestyle Habits	How This Affects Me	Why This Aspect Is Limited
Relaxation			
Exercise			
Sleep			
Nutrition			
Social Support			
Humor			
Other			

The most important affects of moodiness on my lifestyle is _____

_____

Reducing Stress

Stress can intensify your feelings of depression. Following are some of the stress-management techniques that you can use to decrease your deflated mood. Complete the table below to identify stress-management techniques that might be effective for you.

Aspects of My Lifestyle	Tried and Liked It. Why Do You Like It?	Have Not Tried It. Why Haven't You?	Tried and Do Not Like it. Why Not?
Relaxation – *Find a quiet place to relax, meditate, do yoga, listen to soothing music, guided imagery, deep breathing.*			
Exercise – *Regular exercise, physical activity like gardening, walking/jogging, aerobic exercising, yoga, martial arts.*			
Sleep – *Before bed, have a nighttime sleep routine, avoid eating, drinking, and physical activity, and make sure the room conditions are comfortable.*			
Nutrition – *Eating nutritional well-balanced meals, which enhances your ability to fight moodiness.*			
Social Support – *Confide in and talk with trusted friends and family about your moodiness.*			
Humor – *Tell and enjoy audience appropriate jokes, relate funny stories to others, watch humorous television shows or movies.*			
Other			

Managing Moods

External Causes of Moodiness

Moodiness develops from a variety of external causes. By becoming more aware of some of the external causes of depressed moods, you can develop a plan to overcome them. For each of the following items in the next two pages, place an X over the spot on the line that you think describes your level of mood alterations.

Loneliness   Sunny 0-------------5-------------10 Gloomy

Explain _____

_____

Lack of social support   Sunny 0-------------5-------------10 Gloomy

Explain _____

_____

Recent stressful life experiences   Sunny 0-------------5-------------10 Gloomy

Explain _____

_____

Family history of depression   Sunny 0-------------5-------------10 Gloomy

Explain _____

_____

Marital or relationship problems   Sunny 0-------------5-------------10 Gloomy

Explain _____

_____

Poor self-esteem   Sunny 0-------------5-------------10 Gloomy

Explain _____

_____

(Continued on the next page)

External Causes of Moodiness (Continued)

	Sunny		Gloomy

Financial strain　　　　　　　　　　0----------------------5-------------------------------10

Explain_____

_____

　　　　　　　　　　　　　　　　　　Sunny　　　　　　　　　　　　　　Gloomy

Early childhood trauma or abuse　　0----------------------5-------------------------------10

Explain_____

_____

　　　　　　　　　　　　　　　　　　Sunny　　　　　　　　　　　　　　Gloomy

Alcohol or drug abuse　　　　　　　0----------------------5-------------------------------10

Explain_____

_____

　　　　　　　　　　　　　　　　　　Sunny　　　　　　　　　　　　　　Gloomy

Unemployed or not satisfied with job　0----------------------5-------------------------------10

Explain_____

_____

　　　　　　　　　　　　　　　　　　Sunny　　　　　　　　　　　　　　Gloomy

Health problems or chronic pain　　　　　　　　　　　　　　　　　　　　　　0------
---------------------------5---------------------------------10

Explain_____

_____

　　　　　　　　　　　　　　　　　　Sunny　　　　　　　　　　　　　　Gloomy

Loss of loved one(s)　　　　　　　　　　　　　　　　　　　　　　　　　　　0------
---------------------------5---------------------------------10

Explain_____

_____

　　　　　　　　　　　　　　　　　　Sunny　　　　　　　　　　　　　　Gloomy

Other　　　　　　　　　　　　　　　0----------------------5-------------------------------10

Explain_____

_____

Managing Moods

When My Life Was Better

At one point in time, your life might have been better than it is now. Reflect about on how aspects of your life were working when life was better. Think back to a time when you felt like your life was more interesting, engaging and/or satisfying than it is now. Answer the following questions based on the image you have in your mind.

Describe a time in your life when your life was more interesting, engaging and/or satisfying than it is now. Where were you? What were you doing?

___
___
___
___

What were your intimate relationships like?

___
___
___
___

What were your friendships like?

___
___
___
___

Where were you working, and what motivated you in the work you were doing?

___
___
___
___

(Continued on the next page)

When My Life Was Better *(Continued)*

In what types of leisure and community activities were you interested and engaged?
_____
_____
_____
_____

How was your personal health different?
_____
_____
_____
_____

How were your lifestyle habits different?
_____
_____
_____
_____

What are the major differences between then and now in your life?
_____
_____
_____
_____

What can you do to make your current life better?
_____
_____
_____
_____

Managing Moods

My Feelings

Answer the following prompts to further explore your feelings and the extent of your moodiness. If any of the following are not issues for you, write "not my issue."

Complete these sentence starters:

My persistent sad, anxious, or *empty* mood _____

_____

_____

My sudden swings in mood _____

_____

_____

My feelings of hopelessness or pessimism _____

_____

_____

My feelings of guilt, worthlessness, or helplessness _____

_____

_____

My loss of interest/pleasure in hobbies and activities that were once enjoyed, including sex ____

_____

_____

My changes in energy level _____

_____

_____

My difficulty concentrating, remembering, or making decisions _____

_____

_____

(Continued on the next page)

My Feelings *(Continued)*

My changes in sleep patterns _____
_____
_____

My appetite and/or weight loss, or overeating and weight gain _____
_____
_____

My thoughts of death or suicide or actual suicide attempts _____
_____
_____

My restlessness _____
_____
_____

My irritability_____
_____
_____

My changes in thinking _____
_____
_____

My risk-taking behavior _____
_____
_____

My _____
_____
_____

Building Resilience

When people are able to deal with negative events and changes in their lives, they are said to be resilient. Resiliency is the ability to bounce back. Resilient people can adapt in the face of adversity, trauma, loss and many other forms of stress. Following are some of the ways to build resiliency. Journal about how you will accomplish each one.

I will make more connections by …

___

___

___

I will identify the types of events that cause me the most stress …

___

___

___

I will be more hopeful by …

___

___

___

I will develop some short-term personal or professional goals to achieve including …

___

___

___

I will find ways to learn more about myself by …

___

___

___

I will take care of myself better by …

___

___

___

Hiding and Mirroring Emotions

What do you see when you look in the mirror? Often times what we see is an illusion and not reality because you hide your emotions from others. You have two mirrors below.

Pretend you are looking in the mirror on the left. Draw a picture of how others see you.

Now move to the second mirror on the right. Draw a picture of how you see yourself.

HOW OTHERS SEE ME	**HOW I SEE MYSELF**

What are the differences in the two mirrors? _____
_____
_____

Managing Moods

Just Do It!

When people feel sad, they often shy away from people and activities. They want to wait until these feelings pass to get back to normal daily activities. This often leads to a continued downward spiral. It is often better to do whatever activities you enjoy. Encourage and motivate yourself to be with people and continue engaging in activities. In the spaces that follow, write about or draw four fun activities you stopped doing when you feel down.

ACTIVITY 1	**ACTIVITY 2**
ACTIVITY 3	**ACTIVITY 4**

Which activities do you enjoy most? _____

Feeling Moody

It helps to identify how we appear to others, and how we behave, when we are moody. To begin, circle the "moody" words in the word search. HINT: The 2-word "Search Words" have a letter between them.

A	S	D	F	G	U	N	R	E	A	C	H	A	B	L	E	H	J	K	L
Z	X	C	V	B	N	M	Q	W	M	I	S	E	R	A	B	L	E	E	S
G	R	M	P	T	Y	U	I	S	A	D	O	P	M	N	B	V	C	A	T
R	E	L	O	K	J	H	A	U	H	G	F	D	S	A	O	I	U	U	R
O	Y	T	U	P	R	E	W	L	Z	C	A	S	N	O	T	B	I	N	E
U	C	A	T	P	E	T	U	L	A	N	T	U	M	B	E	C	R	A	S
C	S	X	Y	U	S	E	V	E	I	L	L	E	H	U	M	O	R	P	S
H	A	N	X	I	O	U	S	N	S	T	E	K	R	L	P	E	I	P	E
Y	D	U	T	E	B	B	G	E	R	G	J	I	O	H	E	N	T	R	D
L	A	I	P	T	W	A	B	L	K	A	S	D	T	H	R	Y	A	O	N
M	G	L	F	R	O	W	N	Y	O	U	R	I	E	Y	A	E	B	A	L
T	L	T	A	A	R	N	D	N	O	O	E	R	M	A	M	A	L	C	O
N	U	L	Y	N	T	N	B	A	D	E	M	O	O	D	E	M	E	H	N
Y	M	B	R	O	H	S	D	K	Y	A	N	Y	D	J	N	A	C	K	G
Y	U	O	L	I	L	S	H	S	U	L	K	S	O	P	T	H	I	B	A
A	N	G	R	Y	E	A	I	R	L	E	L	E	A	N	A	D	J	L	F
E	Y	N	N	O	S	M	A	S	U	N	S	T	O	B	L	E	N	E	A
K	B	O	R	P	S	L	A	Y	S	C	E	H	S	S	A	S	P	E	C
A	K	S	C	H	I	E	N	E	S	E	J	Y	G	O	S	E	T	O	E
T	H	C	R	O	S	S	E	W	O	O	G	R	U	M	P	Y	D	W	R

Think about times when you are moody.
Check your "top 10" of how you are feeling at those times when you are moody.
Then, check your "top 10" of how you think you appear to others at those moody times.

Search Words	How I Feel	How I Appear to Others
Angry		
Anxious		
Bad mood		
Cross		
Frowny		
Gloomy		
Glum		
Grouchy		
Grumpy		
Ill humor		
Long face		
Miserable		

Search Words	How I Feel	How I Appear to Others
Mope		
Morose		
Petulant		
Pouty		
Stressed		
Sulk		
Sullen		
Temperamental		
Unapproachable		
Unreachable		
Unstable		
Worthless		

Managing Moods

A Letter to Me

Write a letter from the current you to the future you, fifteen years from now. What good advice do you have for the future you?

Dear _____,

_____
_____
_____
_____
_____
_____
_____
_____
_____
_____
_____
_____
_____
_____
_____
_____
_____
_____
_____
_____
_____
_____
_____
_____

Sincerely, _____

"To Understand Me..."

> *To understand me, you have to meet me and be around me.*
> *And then, only if I'm in a good mood — don't meet me in a bad mood.*
> ~ Avril Lavigne

What does this quote mean to you?

_____
_____
_____
_____

How do people relate to you when you are in a good mood?

_____
_____
_____
_____

How do people relate to you when you are in a bad mood?

_____
_____
_____
_____

When you're in a bad mood, what can you say to them to help them understand?

_____
_____
_____
_____

Remember that you have many options for coping with your moodiness, and you do not have to suffer alone. There are people around you to support you in your efforts to overcome your moodiness in a helpful, healthy way! You just need to let them.

Managing Moods

MODULE II
Effects of Moodiness

There are wounds that never show on the body that are deeper and more hurtful than anything that bleeds.

~ Laurell K. Hamilton

Name _____

Date _____

Managing Moods

Effects of Moodiness Scale
Introduction and Directions

One way to look at the effects that moodiness has on your life is to be aware of the symptoms of moodiness in four major areas of your life:

- Health
- Relationships
- Work
- Social Activities

This assessment contains 32 statements designed to help you explore how your moodiness may be affecting each life area. Read each of the statements and decide the statement that describes you. If the statement does describe you, circle the number in the YES column next to that item. If the statement does not describe you, circle the number in the NO column next to that item.

In the following example, the circled 1 indicates the statement does not describe the person completing the inventory:

Often, in my personal life …	YES	NO
I am unusually fatigued …	2	1

This is not a test. Since there are no right or wrong answers, do not spend too much time thinking about your answers. Be sure to respond to every statement.

Turn to the next page and begin.

Managing Moods

Effects of Moodiness Scale

Often, in my personal life …	YES	NO
I am unusually fatigued	2	1
I have more mysterious aches and pains than usual	2	1
I have a huge appetite - or - I have no appetite	2	1
I have insomnia	2	1
I sleep too much	2	1
I increase my substance use	2	1
I feel extremely stressed	2	1
I have no energy	2	1

H – TOTAL = _____

Often, in my relationships …	YES	NO
I have withdrawn from significant people in my life	2	1
I am not interested in sexual relations	2	1
I am not satisfied with anything others say or do	2	1
I don't have a desire to see my friends	2	1
I am inattentive to my significant others	2	1
I don't want to engage in activities with anyone	2	1
I don't feel intimate with others	2	1
I am unresponsive in my closest relationships	2	1

R – TOTAL = _____

(Continued on the next page)

Effects of Moodiness Scale *(Continued)*

Often, at work …	YES	NO
I am not doing my job well	2	1
I have lost interest in the work I do	2	1
I've lost my ambition	2	1
I'm not inspired by what I do for a living	2	1
I feel as if I'm under too much pressure	2	1
I seem to be just going through the motions	2	1
I miss work a lot	2	1
I withdraw or overreact when I am criticized	2	1

W – TOTAL = _____

Often, when it comes to social activities …	YES	NO
I don't engage in them	2	1
I have a hard time experiencing pleasure	2	1
I withdraw because I am afraid of how I'll act	2	1
I just do not want to see anyone	2	1
I get frustrated when I have free time on my hands	2	1
I have low energy levels	2	1
I don't have fun, no matter what I'm doing or who I'm with	2	1
I have lost interest in activities I have always enjoyed	2	1

S – TOTAL = _____

Go to the Scoring Directions on the next page

Managing Moods

Effects of Moodiness Scale Scoring Directions

The assessment you just completed is designed to measure the effects of moodiness on various aspects of your life. For each of the sections on the previous pages, count the scores you circled. Put that total on the line marked TOTAL at the end of each section.

Then, transfer your total to the space below:

        H = HEALTH   TOTAL _____

        R = RELATIONSHIPS TOTAL _____

        W = WORK   TOTAL _____

        S = SOCIAL ACTIVITES TOTAL _____

To get your Grand Total, add your four scores together. _____

Profile Interpretation

Individual Scale Score	Grand Total	Result	Indications
8 to 10 in any single area	32 to 42 for your Grand Total	Low	Low scores indicate that you are not being affected too much by your moodiness. Complete the following exercises to reduce the effects even more.
11 to 13 in any single area	43 to 53 for your Grand Total	Moderate	Moderate scores indicate that you are being somewhat affected by your moodiness. Complete the following exercises to reduce the effects.
14 to 16 in any single area	54 to 64 for your Grand Total	High	High scores indicate that you are being greatly affected by your moodiness. Complete the following exercises to reduce the effects even more.

Individual Scale Descriptions

HEALTH – People scoring high on this scale tend to feel the effect of moodiness on their personal health. They have limited energy, don't feel like eating, and may even have trouble sleeping.

RELATIONSHIPS – People scoring high on this scale tend to feel the effects of moodiness on their relationships with others. They lose contact with friends, withdraw from social situations, and have a hard time showing intimacy.

WORK – People scoring high on this scale tend to feel the effect of moodiness on the work they do. They lose interest in work, feel pressured to get their work done, and lose their ambition.

SOCIAL ACTIVITES – People scoring high on this scale tend to feel the effect of moodiness in participation of social activities. They lose interest in being out with other people, have a hard time experiencing pleasure, and generally lack the energy to participate in social and recreational activities.

GRAND TOTAL – High scores on all four scales indicates that the person is affected greatly by moodiness. The following pages will be helpful to everyone, no matter how they scored.

Effects of Moodiness

My Personal Health

The effects of moodiness on your personal health are not always obvious. Some of the effects are more pronounced than others. In the table below, identify all of the health issues you experience related to your moodiness.

Lifestyle	How I React When I'm Moody	How I am Affected	How can I Cope Better
Example: Food choices	I eat sweets.	I feel sick and get very tired and then gain weight.	I could eat other foods that aren't so sugary.
Food Choices			
Exercise			
Sleep			
Relaxation			
Professional Help			
Spirituality			
Other			

If you are experiencing symptoms of moodiness that are affecting your health, it is time to consult professional medical help.

Managing Moods

Managing My Moodiness

Coping with moodiness can be made easier by taking care of yourself. For each of these sentence starters, write how you can manage your moodiness by taking care of yourself.

I can eat less refined sugar by _____
_____
_____

I can eat a better well-balanced diet by _____
_____
_____

I can get more exercise by _____
_____
_____

I can enjoy more sunlight (safely) by _____
_____
_____

I can take time for quiet self-reflection by _____
_____
_____

I can take time for a healing therapy by _____
_____
_____

I can get the right amount of sleep for my needs by_____
_____
_____

(Continued on the next page)

Managing My Moodiness *(Continued)*

I can journal my thoughts by _____
_____
_____

I can take time to meditate by _____
_____
_____

I can find professional help by _____
_____
_____

I can let my creative juices flow by _____
_____
_____

I can explore my religious and/or spirituality practices by _____
_____
_____

I can take my medications regularly by _____
_____
_____

I can _____
_____
_____
_____

Managing Moods

Let's Get Physical

Engaging in physical activity has been shown to greatly reduce the effects of moodiness. Think about the amount of physical activity you participate in each week.

Physical Activity	How Much Time Devoted Per Week	How This Helps Me	If I Don't, Why Not?
Exercise			
Ride a bicycle			
Walk, jog and/or walk a pet			
Play sports			
Join a gym			
Engage in aerobic activities			
Lift weights			
Practice yoga, tai chi, etc.			
Aerobics or dance classes			
Swim or Aquatic exercise			
Work around the house			
Take stairs			
Stretch			
Other			
Other			
Other			

When completed, go back to the list above and put a check by the activities you are willing to do more regularly.

Effects of Moodiness

Relationships

Your moodiness may be affecting your relationships with significant others in your life. In the table below, explore how you believe your moodiness is affecting your relationships.

Relationship	Signs of My Moodiness	How It Affects This Person
Partner Name _John_	I "snap" at him when he asks me a perfectly logical question.	He feels like he has to walk on "eggshells" around me.
Partner Name _____ Name _____ Name _____		
Child Name _____ Name _____ Name _____		
Friend Name _____ Name _____ Name _____		
Neighbor Name _____ Name _____ Name _____		
Co-workers or Boss Name _____ Name _____ Name _____		
Others Name _____ Name _____ Name _____		

How important is it to you to reduce the impact of your moodiness on these relationships?
_____

How will you do it? _____
_____

© 2014 WHOLE PERSON ASSOCIATES, 101 W. 2ND ST., SUITE 203, DULUTH MN 55802 • 800-247-6789

Managing Moods

The Impact on My Relationships

Coping with moodiness can be made easier by being aware of what is happening due to your moodiness and then, ideally, figuring out what to do about it. For each sentence starter below, write about the impact of your moodiness on your relationships.

_____ is getting angry at me and _____

_____ is staying away from me and _____

_____ is saying it is all in my head and _____

_____ is getting tired of me and my moodiness, and _____

_____ excludes me from _____

_____ doesn't even try to understand me, instead _____

I think I need to _____

Effects of Moodiness

Involving Family & Friends

Having the support of trusted family members and trusted friends can be extremely helpful in managing moods. This support might even strengthen your relationships with them and others. In the table below, write about the ways that your friends and family could support you and how you could ask for their support, explaining how they can help you.

Ways People Can Support Me	Family and Friends Names or Initials	Specifically, or Example of How They Can Support Me	How I Can Ask for Support
Be more tolerant			
Be more patient			
Stop avoiding me			
Provide me with alone time			
Listen to me			
Learn about my mood problems			
Tell me when I am being difficult			
Other			
Other			
Other			

In the second column, place a check by the people you trust enough to explain your moodiness issues and then ask for support.

© 2014 WHOLE PERSON ASSOCIATES, 101 W. 2ND ST., SUITE 203, DULUTH MN 55802 • 800-247-6789

Managing Moods

Moodiness At Work

Your moodiness may be affecting your performance at work, your ability to move up in an organization, and ultimately your career development. In the table below, identify all of the ways your moodiness is affecting your performance on a job.

People I Deal with at Work	How I Am Affected	How I Can Do Better
Example: Co-Workers	People are starting to avoid me because I am so negative.	I could try to start looking at the bright side, and avoid saying anything negative.
Co-Workers		
Supervisors		
Customers		
People I Supervise		
Vendors		
Other		
Other		
Other		

Effects of Moodiness

Managing My Moodiness at Work

Coping with moodiness can be made easier by taking care of yourself in the workplace.

Tips

- Wake up in plenty of time to have a good breakfast and not feel rushed or frustrated due to family responsibilities or traffic on the way to work.
- Arrive at work early to prepare for your day.
- Take time off if needed.
- Do not take on more than you can handle.
- Delegate any responsibilities that you are able to.
- Break tasks into small tasks to avoid feeling overwhelmed.
- Take breaks when you can. Relax. Listen to relaxing music if you can.
- Be aware of how your thinking influences how you feel and how you behave.
- Access an Employee Assistance Program if one is available.

Which of the tips will you be able to implement immediately? How will you do so?

_____
_____
_____

What types of responsibilities could you delegate at work?

_____
_____
_____

What types of tasks are you given that seem overwhelming?

_____
_____
_____

How could you break these tasks down into smaller steps so you are not so overwhelmed?

_____
_____
_____

Managing Moods

Social Activities

When you are feeling moody, your first instinct may be to isolate yourself from others. This is probably one of the worst things you can do. Interacting with other people can be of tremendous help to you. When you are by yourself, you tend to sit and dwell too much on the negative. Instead, think about some of the ways that you can continue engaging in social activities.

Social Activities	Social Activities I Enjoy	How They Help Me
Example: *Sports-Related*	*I like going to high school basketball games.*	*I see other parents in the neighborhood and we chat.*
Sports-Related		
Religious / Spiritual		
Creative		
Educational		
Cultural		
Other		
Other		
Other		

What types of activities have you given up because of your changeable moods?
_____
_____
_____

Would you consider resuming any of these activities? _____ When? _____

Effects of Moodiness

Get Involved Socially

Coping with moods can affect your interest in all daily activities, especially social endeavors. The most common reaction is to withdraw from other people and activities. When you begin to limit your social and recreational pursuits, you begin to physically shut down. Think about the following sentence starters as they relate to your participation in social and recreational activities.

When I feel moody,

I want to be by myself because _____
_____
_____

I don't feel like being sociable so I _____
_____
_____

I miss taking part in social and recreational activities such as_____
_____
_____

I feel bad later because I missed out on _____
_____
_____

I worry that I give others the impression that _____
_____
_____

I feel as if I am _____
_____
_____

Managing Moods

Activating Events

When people feel depressed, they often shy away from people and activities. They want to wait until the moodiness passes to return to normal daily activities. This often leads to a continued downward spiral. The person's thinking often triggers this downward spiral. Following is an explanation of how negative thoughts keep people from engaging in social and recreational activities. The good news is that you are able to reverse these negative thoughts and turn them into positive ones.

Some Tactics

Identify the activating event – In this case, it is your negative thinking about engaging in social and recreational activities. This technique will work for any activating event in your life. What is an event coming up in which you would like to attend or engage? This could be a social event, party, dinner out with a friend, sports events, child's school play, etc.

_____

Identify your negative thoughts – Identify the negative thoughts that occur as a result of your beliefs about engaging in social and recreational activities. These negative thoughts are often irrational as they are inconsistent with reality. Identify your negative thoughts below:

_____
_____
_____

Identify the consequences of your negative thinking. What do you do in response to your negative thoughts?

_____
_____
_____

Now you need to dispute those thoughts! Several questions you need to ask yourself:

How am I making a pessimistic prediction of the future?

_____

In what ways am I jumping to conclusions?

_____

What is the basis in reality for my thinking?

_____

When or how am I giving in to "should statements" (*You should stay home because....*)?

_____

You can challenge all of your negative thinking with this method!

Effects of Moodiness

Reverse Your Negative Thinking

*"We either make ourselves miserable or we make ourselves strong.
The amount of work is the same."*
~ Carlos Castaneda

In order to make yourself strong rather than miserable, you need to convert your negative thinking into more positive thinking. One way to do this is to simply recognize what is happening in your own mind. In this case, attend to the stream of thoughts that go through your head when you are moody. Look at an example:

- **Negative thoughts in my head:** "Nobody loves me!" and "I'll never find someone with whom to share my life."
- **Feelings that follow:** Low self-esteem, loneliness, fear and/or hopelessness.
- **Where is the evidence?** There is no evidence. "I do have people who love me." and "I have plenty of time to meet someone special."
- **How I could reverse my thinking:** "I am worthy of being loved." and "I will find someone if I don't give up and if I continue engaging in social activities, where I can meet new people!"

Now that you have the formula for successfully reversing your negative thinking, you try it below:

Negative Thoughts That Often Run Through My Head	Feelings That Follow	Where Is the Evidence?	How I Could Reverse Them

With whom do you usually have negative thoughts? Why? What can you do about it?

_____

_____

When and where do you usually have negative thoughts? Why? What can you do about it?

_____

_____

Managing Moods

Positive Activity Schedule

When one feels *down*, there is a strong tendency to stop engaging in positive emotional events. It is important to have positive experiences that build positive emotions. Rather than waiting until you feel "in the mood," begin engaging in enjoyable activities. It may help to motivate you to have a schedule of positive activities for the coming week. In the table below, identify the positive events and activities in which you can become involved with.

Days of the Week	Positive Events and Activities	What I Can Gain from Them
Monday		
Tuesday		
Wednesday		
Thursday		
Friday		
Saturday		
Sunday		

How often can you engage in these activities?

_____

_____

Effects of Moodiness

I Have Choices

"I have the choice of being constantly active and happy, or introspectively passive and sad. Or, I can go mad by ricocheting in between."

~ Sylvia Plath

What does this quote mean to you?
_____
_____
_____

What is the advantage of being active and distracted? _____
_____
_____
_____

Give an example and the results. _____
_____
_____
_____

What is the disadvantage of being active and distracted? _____
_____
_____
_____

Give an example and the results._____
_____
_____
_____

If you are willing, share examples with others in the room.

Managing Moods

MODULE III
Mood Triggers

*That is all I want in life:
for this pain to seem purposeful.*

~ Elizabeth Wurtzel

Name _____

Date _____

Mood Triggers Scale
Introduction and Directions

Moodiness is caused by a variety of external and internal causes, or triggers. Some of these triggers are external and some are internally motivated. By becoming more aware of some of these causes of moodiness, you can better develop a plan for overcoming them.

However, sometimes there are no triggers at all – moodiness just happens.

Read each statement carefully and decide if the statement is related to your moodiness or not. If the statement affects your mood **A Lot**, circle the number 3 next to the statement in that column. If it affects your mood **Some**, circle the number 2 next to the statement in that column. If it has **No Effect**, circle the number 1 next to the statement in that column. Pay no attention to the numbers; read only the column headings. Complete all of the items before going back to score the assessment.

In the following example, the circled 2 indicates that the statement has **some** effect on the person completing the scale.

External factors that trigger my moodiness:	A Lot	Some	No Effect
Loneliness	3	2	1

This is not a test and there are no right or wrong answers. Do not spend too much time thinking about your answers. Your initial response will be the most true for you. Be sure to respond to every statement.

Turn to the next page and begin.

Managing Moods

Mood Triggers Scale

External factors that trigger my moodiness:	A Lot	Some	No Effect
Loneliness	3	2	1
Lack of social support	3	2	1
Stage of life crisis	3	2	1
Family problems	3	2	1
Recent stressful life experiences	3	2	1
Family history of mental health issues	3	2	1
Marital or relationship problems	3	2	1
Homeless	3	2	1
Financial problems	3	2	1
Caregiving	3	2	1
Hospitalization	3	2	1
Early childhood trauma or abuse	3	2	1
Alcohol or drug abuse	3	2	1
Criminal issues	3	2	1
Health problems or chronic pain	3	2	1
Significant personal losses	3	2	1
Job related issues	3	2	1
Legal problems	3	2	1
Insecurity about the future	3	2	1
Parenthood issues	3	2	1
Break-up or divorce	3	2	1
Feeling bad for no known reason at all	3	2	1

E - TOTAL = _____

(Continued on the next page)

Mood Triggers Scale *(Continued)*

Internal factors that trigger my moodiness:	A Lot	Some	No Effect
Inability to forgive	3	2	1
Fear	3	2	1
Loss of meaning in life	3	2	1
Shame and/or embarrassment	3	2	1
Low self-esteem	3	2	1
Feelings of being a victim	3	2	1
Inability to realize potential	3	2	1
Feelings of hopelessness	3	2	1
Self-doubt	3	2	1
Negative self-talk	3	2	1
Inability to reach goals	3	2	1
Feeling that there's something wrong with me.	3	2	1
Fault-finding with myself	3	2	1
Lack of self-confidence	3	2	1
Feelings of being blamed	3	2	1
Feelings of failure	3	2	1
Focus on the negative	3	2	1
Feelings of guilt	3	2	1
Feelings of being different from everyone else	3	2	1
Feelings of being judged	3	2	1
Feeling like life is not fair	3	2	1
Possible chemical imbalance or health issues	3	2	1

I - TOTAL = _____

Go to the Scoring Directions on the next page

Managing Moods

Mood Triggers Scale
Scoring Directions

Add the numbers you circled on both scales and write those scores on the lines marked TOTAL. Then, transfer those totals to the spaces below:

E = EXTERNAL TOTAL _____

I = INTERNAL TOTAL _____

Profile Interpretation

Individual Scale Score	Result	Indications
22 to 36	Low	Low scores indicate that you do not experience moodiness due to these types of triggers.
37 to 51	Moderate	Moderate scores indicate that you experience some moodiness due to these types of triggers.
52 to 66	High	High scores indicate that you experience a great deal of moodiness due to these types of triggers.

No matter how you scored, low, moderate or high, you will benefit from these exercises.

By completing the activities that follow, you will better understand the impact of internal and external triggers in your life.

Scale Descriptions

External – People scoring high on this scale tend to experience moodiness as a result of occurrences in their environment like death, unemployment, illness, and financial crises.

Internal – People scoring high on this scale tend to experience moodiness as a result of the feelings that are generated from their own negative thinking. They tend to think like victims and focus on the negative aspects of any situation.

Mood Triggers

My Mood Patterns

It is helpful to think about how to deal with your patterns of moodiness. Think about when you begin to feel moody and answer the questions that follow:

Do you get moody at certain times of the year? In which seasons does it intensify?
_____
_____
_____

What is the association between the occurrence of stressful events and the onset of your moodiness? What are examples of these events?
_____
_____
_____

Describe the situations in which your moodiness is intensified.
_____
_____
_____

How does the weather affect you moodiness? What type of weather and how does it affect you?
_____
_____
_____

Is your moodiness connected to your use of drinking and/or substance use? Describe.
_____
_____
_____

How does your moodiness seem to come upon you? For no reason at all? As a result of an event or episode? Explain.
_____
_____
_____

Managing Moods

My Treatment History

People who experience moodiness and mood swings often see medical professionals for treatment. It is important to track your treatment history to see which treatments are working and which are not. In the table below, write your prescribed medications as well as non-prescribed medications. Make extra copies of this form if needed.

Medication and How Often?	Reason for Taking Med?	Date Started?	How Helpful?	Side Effects?

Mood Triggers

Early Warning Signs

The symptoms of moodiness might come and go throughout your life. This is okay if you know how to manage your symptoms effectively. To do this you need to recognize your symptoms. If you are able to notice early changes in your mood, you can take action. In the table below, explore how you usually feel and then how you feel when you are beginning to experience a mood change.

Symptom	How I Usually Feel When I'm Not Moody	How I Feel When I Am Becoming Moody
Example: General mood	I am pretty optimistic.	I see the negative side of everything.
General mood		
Hope about my future		
Social activity		
Sleeping habits		
Eating habits		
Self-esteem		
Ability to concentrate		
Ability to rest		

(Continued on the next page)

Managing Moods

Early Warning Signs *(Continued)*

Symptom	How I Usually Feel When I'm Not Moody	How I Feel When I Am Becoming Moody
Energy level		
Intimacy level		
Decision making		
Thoughts about suicide		
Concern for myself		
Interest in having fun. Laughing.		
Self-confidence		
Concern for significant others		
Ability to tolerate frustration		
Stress Management		
Other: _____		

I'm Overwhelmed

Being overwhelmed can definitely affect your moodiness.
Below are some tips in feeling less overwhelmed:

- Try to stop looking at the larger picture, as it can exhaust you before you even begin.
- Change the way you look at the problem or task. Break larger tasks down into smaller ones that can be accomplished easily. This will provide you with the motivation to continue.
- Listen to the negative self-talk in your own mind. Be aware of negative thoughts like "I can't do this" and "I should quit." Change this negative thinking to positive thoughts like "I can do this" and "It may not be perfect, but I can accomplish this."
- When you begin to feel overwhelmed, walk away for a while and relax, then come back to the task.
- Do one thing at a time; work through the process in a systematic manner.

What Overwhelms Me	How It Overwhelms Me	What I Can Do About It
Example: Too much to do in one day.	I become anxious and am constantly looking at the clock.	Prioritize and do as much as I can.

Managing Moods

Exercise

Exercising is one of the best ways to reduce the effect of moodiness once it has been triggered. When using exercise as a way to reduce your moodiness, keep several things in mind:

- Check with your physician first.
- Begin now and continue on a regular schedule.
- Choose activities that will reduce moodiness but not be so strenuous that they cause you stress.
- Select activities that are continuous and rhythmic in nature.
- Be wary of competitive sports for they can cause undue stress.
- Start slowly and build up endurance over time.

In the spaces that follow, identify types of exercises you have tried. State how you felt before engaging in them and how you felt afterwards.

Form of Exercising	How I Felt Before	How I Felt Afterwards
Walking		
Jogging		
Riding a Bicycle		
Dancing		
Yoga		
Swimming		
Water Aerobics		
Skiing		
Gardening		
Working Around the House		
Weight Lifting		
Aerobics		
Martial Arts		
Other		

You Are What You Eat

In the case of moodiness, you often really are what you eat. A proper food regimen is critical in balancing your emotional health. During moody periods, people usually eat unbalanced snacks or meals. One way of managing external triggers to moodiness is to maintain a well-balanced way of eating.

TIPS:
- Reduce your fat intake
- Reduce your alcohol intake
- Reduce your use of caffeine
- Reduce the amount of sugar you eat and drink
- Eat more fruits and vegetables
- Eat a lot of grains (rye, oats, wheat, etc.)
- Eat protein-rich foods (beans and peas, lean beef, low-fat cheese, milk, poultry, soy products, yogurt)
- Eat plenty of fish
- When you go to a fast-food chain, find one that has healthy foods as well.

What types of foods do you eat too much of when you are in a bad mood?

_____
_____
_____
_____

What types of foods do you not eat enough of when you are in a bad mood?

_____
_____
_____
_____

What changes can you make to practice a well-balanced way of eating, moody or not?

_____
_____
_____
_____

Managing Moods

Relaxation Techniques

Relaxation techniques can provide immediate benefits when you begin to feel your mood changing. Consider a variety of techniques that may help you relax. Below are a few. There are many more relaxation techniques may be found on reliable Internet sources.

Deep Breathing – Deep breathing involves inhaling slowly through your nose (you should notice your abdomen going up and down) and exhaling through your mouth. Repeat this process by continuing to take long, slow deep breaths that raise and lower your abdomen. Continue this process for at least five to ten minutes or until your mood has lightened. Now you try it. Then describe below how you felt during the deep breathing exercise.

_____

_____

_____

_____

Light – Light can be extremely beneficial in reversing a bad mood. Try to spend at least a half an hour per day outside in the sunlight. You can simply walk or relax in a lounge chair. Remember that too much sunlight can be bad for your skin, so be careful. You may also want to ensure that the rooms in your house are well lit. Then describe below how you felt during your time in the sunshine and light.

_____

_____

_____

_____

Meditation – Meditation can help you to focus your attention on one thing at a time. For example, you could take a few minutes and gaze at an object of your choice (a candle, cup, flower, etc.) at your eye level. Gaze at the object for a few minutes. Note its size, shape and color. If you become distracted, simply return your gaze to the object. You could also count your breaths by counting one for each time you inhale and two when you exhale. Continue counting your breaths until you reach ten, and then begin again with one. Try it and describe below what happened to you - the thoughts running through your head - and your mood.

_____

_____

_____

_____

That's Funny

Having a good sense of humor can help to maintain a positive perspective. Humor has been referred to as a natural antidote to moodiness.

Be more playful around other people. How can you be more playful with people in your life?

___

See the funny side or opposite side of every situation. What types of situation could you flip around so that they seem funny?

___

Laugh at situations involving yourself, either when something happens, or later, when you look back on it. If you do something silly, don't be afraid to laugh at yourself. What is an event that happened to you that was funny a while later as you told the story?

___

It is good to laugh with others about situations. Why should you not laugh at other people?

___

Take yourself and life more lightly. Try to stop seeing some situations so seriously. What types of situations do you take way too seriously?

___

Watch humorous movies or television shows. What are your favorites? Compare with others in the room.

___

Managing Moods

When I'm Getting Worse!

As you probably already know, if you are suffering with moodiness, many things can make your mood worse. In the spaces that follow, identify some of the things that make you feel worse.

When I am overwhelmed, I feel worse when _____
_____
_____

When I am isolated, I feel worse when people _____
_____
_____

When I am ignored, I feel worse when people _____
_____
_____

When I am frustrated, I feel worse when _____
_____
_____

When I am ill, I feel worse when people _____
_____
_____

When I'm with _____ I feel worse when _____
_____
_____

To whom can you talk with when you feel worse? _____

Mood Triggers

My Internal Triggers

Some of your internal triggers of moodiness are the result of your thinking. Your thinking can actually influence how you feel! Therefore, you need to be cognizant of how your thinking can be triggering your moodiness. Following are some of the different types of negative thinking patterns that might be affecting how you feel.

Name Calling – In this type of thinking, you attach a negative label to yourself or to others. Examples include "I'm a bad person" or "He's a terrible father." What are some of the labels you call yourself and call others?

_____
_____
_____

Tyranny of "Would" "Should" and "Could" – In this type of thinking, you keep thinking about how things could, should or would have been done. What are some of the "woulds" "shoulds" and/or "coulds" you have for yourself and for other people.

_____
_____
_____

Tuning In – In this type of thinking, you focus on the negative aspects of a situation or aspects about yourself and ignore the positive aspects of the situation or accomplishment. Provide some examples.

_____
_____
_____

Make a Mountain out of a Molehill – In this type of thinking, you blow events and situations out of proportion, often because you lack adequate information. An example of this is when a person forgets to pay a bill, and thinks he is totally inadequate. What types of situations or events trigger this sort of thinking in you?

_____
_____
_____

Make an effort to eliminate these negative patterns from your thinking. It will make a difference!

Managing Moods

Victim Thinking

Because many of the internal triggers of moodiness are the result of your victim thinking, you can control these internal triggers by learning more effective ways of thinking. Here are some of the more effective ways of controlling internal triggers due to victim thinking.

Type	When I Do This	How I Can Control This Type of Thinking
Overthinking – *Example: I am so unsure of myself, I keep thinking and thinking about an issue of any kind.*		
Worrying – *Example: I have such low self-confidence, I continually worry about things, even if they are out of my control.*		
Pessimistic thinking – *Example: I believe that nothing good will ever happen to me.*		
Feelings of being blamed – *Example: I have lost so much faith in myself that I feel like people blame me for anything and everything.*		
Other: _____ _____ _____		

Which of the types above best describes you? Who is a trusted person you can talk with about this, to develop a plan of controlling this internal trigger?

_____

_____

Worry, Worry, Worry

You can become more moody just by worrying about events that may or may not occur in the future. The problem with worrying is that very often the event is not as bad as you imagined it to be and you probably worried for nothing. Even if it is bad, your worrying and/or being out of control usually does not help the situation. Identify those times in your life when you worried more than you needed to.

Events	My Worrying Thoughts	How I Handled It	The Outcome of the Situation	Another Way to Have Handled It
Example: My daughter was late coming home.	I was sure she was in a car accident.	I called her and when she didn't answer, I called the police.	Her phone was off.	If I called her friend she'd have told me they were sitting in the car outside of my house talking.

"If a problem is fixable, if a situation is such that you can do something about it, then there is no need to worry. If it's not fixable, then there is no help in worrying. There is no benefit in worrying whatsoever."

~Dalai Lama XIV

Managing Moods

My Self-Esteem

Moodiness can have an extremely negative effect on how and what you think about yourself and your self-esteem. It can trigger feelings in you so that you believe that you are different from others, or that you feel you can't reach your goals. It can magnify your fears of interacting with others or becoming intimate with people. What and how you think about yourself can have an extremely positive or an extremely negative effect on your moods.

Some ways to boost your self-esteem:

Take part in community activities.

- Activities in which I already engage:
  _____
  _____

- Activities in which I would like to engage:
  _____
  _____

Choose work or a volunteer job that you will enjoy.

- Work I do not enjoy:
  _____
  _____

- Work I enjoy:
  _____
  _____

Participate in activities in which you feel good about yourself.

- Activities in which I am good:
  _____
  _____

- Activities in which I have no natural talents:
  _____
  _____

(Continued on the next page)

My Self-Esteem *(Continued)*

Identify your achievements.

- My best achievement:

  _____
  _____

Think about your career.

- My career accomplishments:

  _____
  _____

- Goals I have for my career:

  _____
  _____

Think about your educational achievements.

- My educational accomplishments:

  _____
  _____

- Goals I have for further education or learning:

  _____
  _____

Express yourself creatively.

- My creative accomplishments:

  _____
  _____

- Goals I have for additional creations:

  _____
  _____

MODULE IV
Roller Coaster Moods

*I know without treatment
I would have never been able to
harness my creativity in such a
successful way.*

~ Patty Duke

Name _____

Date _____

Managing Moods

Roller Coaster Moods Scale
Introduction and Directions

When you feel abnormally elevated, manic-like moods and then, soon after, you feel sad, depressed, down moods, you may be experiencing life like a rollercoaster. The *Roller Coaster Moods Scale* can help you explore, if at times, your moods are like a carousel – whose horses go up and down slightly, or if they are more like a steep, sharply curved roller coaster – very high and then very low. This scale contains 20 statements. Read each of the statements and decide how descriptive the statement is of you. In each of the choices listed, circle the number of your response to the right of each statement.

In the following example, the circled 1 indicates that the statement is not at all descriptive of the person completing the inventory:

4 = Very Descriptive   **3 = Somewhat Descriptive**   **2 = A Little Descriptive**   **1 = Not At All Descriptive**

I have trouble with my sleep patterns	4	3	2	(1)

This is not a test and there are no right or wrong answers. Do not spend too much time thinking about your answers. Your initial response will be the most true for you. Be sure to respond to every statement.

Turn to the next page and begin.

Managing Moods

Roller Coaster Moods Scale

4 = Very Descriptive   3 = Somewhat Descriptive   2 = A Little Descriptive   1 = Not At All Descriptive

I have trouble with my sleep patterns	4	3	2	1
There are times I just can't calm down	4	3	2	1
I am impulsive and rowdy	4	3	2	1
I am loud and laugh at inappropriate times	4	3	2	1
I am preoccupied with sex	4	3	2	1
I have an inflated sense of myself	4	3	2	1
I feel invincible	4	3	2	1
I feel too good	4	3	2	1
I want to keep moving	4	3	2	1
I have sudden, unusual bursts of enthusiasm	4	3	2	1
I seek thrills I don't normally seek	4	3	2	1
I feel "out of control"	4	3	2	1
I am extremely talkative	4	3	2	1
I use poor judgment	4	3	2	1
I spend money foolishly	4	3	2	1
I feel unrealistically ambitious	4	3	2	1
I feel like others are moving in slow motion	4	3	2	1
I notice my ideas race around in my head	4	3	2	1
I have surges of energy	4	3	2	1
I feel very restless	4	3	2	1

TOTAL = _____

Go to the Scoring Directions on the next page

Roller Coaster Moods Scale
Scoring Directions

The assessment you just completed is designed to measure the level of your mood instabilities. Count the scores you circled and place that number on the line marked TOTAL at the end of the assessment. Then, transfer your total to the space below:

MOOD INSTABILITY TOTAL = _____

Profile Interpretation

Scale Score	Result	Indications
20 to 40	Low	Low scores indicate that you exhibit subtle bouts of mood instability with slight ups and downs, like a carousel. Complete the following exercises to maintain and develop even more self-control.
41 to 60	Moderate	Moderate scores indicate that you exhibit more than a modest amount of mood instability, somewhere between the highs and lows of a carousel (slight) and a roller coaster (intense). Complete the following exercises to develop greater self-control.
61 to 80	High	High scores indicate that you exhibit intense bouts of mood instability with highs and lows like a roller coaster. Complete the following exercises to assist you in developing self-control relating to your moods.

Managing Moods

Over-Excited? Frantic? Frenzied? Agitated?

It is helpful to be aware of patterns related to mood swings. Think about when you begin to feel over-excited, frantic, frenzied and or agitated and answer the questions that follow:

What types of changes in your life affect you in the same way as the moods in the title of this page?

_____
_____
_____

What is the association between the occurrence of a stressful event and the onset of these moods? What are these events?

_____
_____
_____

What is the association between the medications you take, or do not take, and the onset of these moods? What is it about your taking of medications that might cause this?

_____
_____
_____

What are the situations (at work, home, community, etc.) in which these moods are intensified? Describe what you are doing when your mood is the most intense?

_____
_____
_____

In what ways do changes in relationships affect or bring on these moods?

_____
_____
_____

In what ways are these moods ever connected to your drinking and/or substance use? Explain.

_____
_____
_____

Early Warning Signs

Roller Coaster Moods

To effectively manage symptoms of being on the high side of a roller coaster, you need to be able to know when those symptoms are emerging. By recognizing early changes in your mood, you can take action to cope more effectively. In the table below, explore how you normally feel and then how you feel when you begin to experience roller coaster highs.

Symptom	Moderate Symptoms	Severe Symptoms
Example: I am impatient	I fidget in the grocery store line and complain to the person behind me.	I am very rude to the people in front of the cashier and around me. Then I leave the cart and walk out.
I am impatient		
I behave impulsively		
Everything seems like a hassle		
I am happier than usual		
I have a very positive outlook		
I am more talkative and talk faster than usual		
I have an inappropriate sense of humor		
I lose my focus easily		
I have more interest in sex		
I can't concentrate on my tasks		

(Continued on the next page)

Managing Moods

Early Warning Signs *(Continued)*

Symptom	Moderate Symptoms	Severe Symptoms
I am overly self-confident		
Any change sounds possible		
I have too many thoughts whirling around		
I am too fidgety to sit still		
I am extremely anxious		
I bite my nails and/or pick my cuticles		
I am more creative than usual		
I have amazing, creative ideas and thoughts		
I am uncomfortable with others		
I lose my train of thought		
I find everyone annoying		
Other _____		

Major Life Decisions

When faced with the early warning signs of a mood instability, it is beneficial to avoid making important life decisions. Decisions that could affect your life, and the lives of those around you, need to be postponed until you feel balanced and in control. In the table below, identify major life decisions that are approaching, and how you will make each of your decisions.

Major Life Decisions	How I Will Go About Making a Decision	How I Will Know I Am in Control
Something Risky – *Example: I am thinking about selling my house and moving to an island.*	*I will talk with my significant other even though I know she may be against it.*	*When I am feeling even-keeled, I will talk to her again and hear her viewpoint. Then we will decide together.*
Something Risky		
Relationships		
Family		
Work Life		
Major Purchase		
Other		

Managing Moods

To Take or Not To Take?

In managing your mood instability, it is important to take your medications regularly, exactly as directed. One of the biggest problems of people who have roller coaster ups-and-downs is that as soon as they feel the pleasant "ups," they think they're okay, and stop taking their meds. They forget that a "high" is usually followed by a crash in mood. If they had cancer, diabetes, or an infection, they would take their meds as long as they needed to, even forever, if necessary. Roller-coaster moods are no different – the meds are important as prescribed. They can be extremely helpful, but they may have unwanted side affects, which can deter people from taking them. People can talk to their physicians and research ways to deal with side affects, and learn which reactions to report immediately.

In the table below, identify all of the medications you have taken and are currently taking; how regularly you take them; the side effects; how you can minimize those side-effects; and how the meds help you. Include both medications prescribed by a physician as well as over-the-counter medicines.

My Medications	Take Regularly?	Side Effects	How I Can Minimize the Side-Effects	How the Meds Help Me

If you have stopped taking them, why?
_____
_____

Have you spoken to your physician about this? If not, why not?
_____
_____

What medication changes/additions do you need to speak about with your physician?
_____
_____

Roller Coaster Moods

Street Drugs and Alcohol

Plain and simple - people with mood instability who use alcohol and street drugs, or abuse prescription medicine, may initially feel better, temporarily, but the symptoms of their mood instability will more likely heighten, return and worsen. In the table below, describe your street drug and alcohol use and how it affects you. The information you write below is confidential and you do not need to share it with anyone, so be honest with yourself.

Type of Street Drug/Alcohol I Use	How Often?	The Effect It Has On Me

Describe and evaluate the effects that drugs and alcohol have on your moodiness.

_____

_____

_____

Managing Moods

Outlets for Excessive Energy

It is often a challenge to find healthy outlets (and we don't mean the outlet mall) for your excessive energy, but it is well worth it. In the table below, explore healthy ways to channel your energy into hobbies, physical and recreational activities, and social activities.

My Healthy Outlets	My Unhealthy Outlets
Recreationally I …	Recreationally I …
Physically I …	Physically I …
Socially I …	Socially I …
Intellectually/Mentally I …	Intellectually/Mentally I …

What can you do to actively engage in more healthy outlets?

Recreationally _____

Physically _____

Socially _____

Intellectually/Mentally _____

Damage-Repair

Roller coaster ups-and-downs will often affect relationships! It is important **to try to stay focused on your relationships.** By keeping your moodiness management goals in mind and reminding yourself that you can work to repair damaged relationships, life will get better! In the table that follows, write about the relationships you have damaged in the midst of mood instabilities.

The Person and Our Relationship	How I Have Damaged the Relationship	How I Can Possibly Repair the Damage
Example: Jane, my spouse	*I verbally abused her by saying some things that no one should say to another person.*	*Talk to a therapist to deal with this issue, apologize to Jane, and promise to stay on my meds. Tell her that I didn't mean what I said.*

Most people will forgive others once or twice. Keeping promises, staying under control and taking meds regularly will ensure the lasting quality of a relationship.

_____

_____

_____

Managing Moods

My WEEKLY Mood Chart

People who experience mood instabilities are often unaware of how quickly and how often their moods go up or down from week to week. A Mood Chart is simply a diary of your mood patterns. This activity will help you to identify when your mood instabilities occur and when you need to implement your coping mechanisms.

Time Frame: _____

Day of the Week	Daily Notes of Mood-Related Issues or Instabilities	Hours Slept	General Mood (Up, down, sad, happy, etc.)
Monday			
Tuesday			
Wednesday			
Thursday			
Friday			
Saturday			
Sunday			

Notes _____
_____

Roller Coaster Moods

My DAILY Mood Chart

People who experience mood instabilities are often unaware of how quickly and how often their moods are unstable, going up and down, from hour to hour. A Mood Chart is simply a diary of your mood patterns. This activity will help you to identify when your mood instabilities occur and when you need to implement your coping mechanisms.

Date _____   Day of the Week _____

Time of the Day	Daily Note of Mood-Related Issues or Instabilities	Hours Slept	General Mood (Up, down, sad, happy, etc.)
7:00 am – 9:00 am			
9:00 am – Noon			
Noon – 3:00 pm			
3:00 pm – 6:00 pm			
6:00 pm – 9:00 pm			
9:00 pm – Midnight			
Midnight – 2:00 am			
2:00 am – 7:00 am			

Notes

_____

_____

_____

Managing Moods

Potential Support Network

Educating (telling about your moods) and involving (asking for support) your significant others, family members and trusted friends about your roller-coaster moods can be unbelievably helpful. In addition, you can involve these important people in your treatment when possible. They can help you spot symptoms, track behaviors, gain perspective, remind you to take meds, go with you to appointments, provide encouraging feedback, and help you make a plan to cope with any future crises.

Who are the significant others, family members and trusted friends with whom you feel safe in confiding, and who can support you? In the table below, identify those people and how they can support you. Some people can support in one way (driving) and others can support in other ways (encouraging). Think about each person and how you can benefit from that person's particular strengths.

Potential Supportive Person	How and What Will I Tell This Person About Me and My Needs	How This Person Can Support Me

Which one of the people above will you contact first? _____

When? _____

My Impulsive Up-Side Behaviors

It is important to identify the impulsive behaviors in which you engage when you are experiencing the upside of your roller-coaster moods. Impulsive behaviors are usually risky behaviors and might include alcohol, drugs, thrills, gambling, abusing meds, etc.

In the table below, explore your behavior.

My Behavior	My Usual Behavior	My Impulsive Behavior
Example: I drive.	I drive carefully – I don't want to get another ticket!	I drive very fast, even if roads are slippery.

TIPS For Overcoming Impulsive Behavior:

Avoid situations that will put you at risk. What are those situations for you? _____
_____
_____

Spend time with people you know and trust. Who are those people? _____
_____
_____

Try to relax. What are some healthy ways that you could relax? _____
_____
_____

Managing Moods

My Social Rhythms

People with roller coaster moods are believed to have overly sensitive biological clocks, the internal timekeepers that regulate circadian rhythms. This clock is easily thrown off by disruptions in your daily pattern of activity, also known as your social rhythms. When these rhythms are stable, the biological rhythms that regulate mood remain stable too. List the times you engage in these activities during the week. Please feel free to reproduce this sheet for additional days.

Today _____

Activity	My Usual Time	My "Down Days" Time	My "Up Days" Time
Example: Get out of bed	7:30 a.m.	11 a.m.	1 or 2 a.m.
Get out of bed			
Interact with anyone			
Have morning coffee/tea/juice			
Have breakfast			
Bathe (if not in the pm)			
Get ready for school/work/family/volunteering/other			
Get to your destination			
Interact with someone			
Have lunch			
Finish work			
Eat dinner			
Watch television news			
Watch additional television/videos			
Evening entertainment			
Eat late night snack			
Bathe (if not in the am)			
Pre-bedtime rituals			
Bedtime			

What did you learn about the stability of your everyday routines? _____

_____

Roller Coaster Moods

Activity vs. Inactivity

In working to manage and/or overcome mood instabilities and their effects, it is important to find the right balance between activity and inactivity. This can be difficult because your body may be telling you that you are too tired to do ANYTHING or it may be telling you to do EVERYTHING! You need to seek balance. Overstimulation by more activities than you can handle easily might trigger an uncomfortable situation.

Aspect of My Life	Activities in Which I'm Involved	Activities I Could Change
Example: spiritual life	*I sing in the choir and I am on two committees that meet each week in the evenings after work.*	*I could eliminate one of the committees to balance my time better.*
Spiritual life		
Community life		
Work life		
Family relationships		
Volunteering		
Time with friends		
Clubs & organizations		
Classes or Training program		
Other		

Which of these changes seems doable? _____

_____

Which of these changes sounds difficult? _____

_____

How can you manage to effect these changes even if it seems difficult? _____

_____

Managing Moods

Predictable and Unpredictable Changes

Changes in your routine can bring on moodiness and mood instabilities. Changes in routine can be either predictable or unpredictable. Predictable changes include getting married in six months, taking a vacation in the summer or starting a new job in a month. These types of changes are usually easier to adjust to. Think about the upcoming changes you know about and how you will prepare to maintain your social rhythms and stability.

Predictable Changes Coming Up in My Routine	How They Will Disrupt My Rhythm	What I Will Do To Adapt

Unpredictable changes include getting fired from your job, a sudden death or an unexpected illness. These types of changes are harder to adjust to. Think back on the unpredicted changes you have experienced and how they affected you and your ability to maintain your social rhythms and stability, and what you learned about yourself.

Unpredictable Changes in My Routine from the Past	How They Affected Me and My Stability and Social Rhythms	What I Learned About Myself to Remember for the Future

Listening

> **Lord Beaverbrook said about Winston Churchill:**
> *"What a creature of strange moods."*

What strange moods do you have?

_____
_____
_____
_____
_____
_____
_____
_____
_____
_____

What is your action plan to ensure that your moods are the way you would like them to be?

_____
_____
_____
_____
_____
_____
_____
_____
_____
_____

Managing Moods

MODULE V
Erasing the Stigma of Mental Health Issues

Mental illness is nothing to be ashamed of, but stigma and bias shames us all.

~ President William J. Clinton

Name _____

Date _____

Managing Moods

Erasing the Stigma of Mental Health Issues
Introduction

A stigma is extreme social disapproval of some type of personal characteristic or a belief that is not considered socially "acceptable." Therefore, stigmas occur when people who have a particular attribute that is considered unwanted by society, are rejected as a result of the attribute. People who experience bouts of moodiness are often judged unfairly to be violent, unpredictable, moody, up and down, sad, explosive, aggressive and/or unstable. These judgments can cause people who experience moodiness to feel devalued as human beings, ostracized from activities, rejected in social situations, stereotyped, minimized in the workplace, and shunned by others. People experiencing the stigma of moodiness often feel extreme physical and psychological distress.

People who stigmatize and/or stereotype others bring about unfair treatment rather than help. This unfair treatment can be very obvious. For example, people make negative comments or laugh. On the other hand, this unfair treatment can be very subtle. For example, people assume that a moody person is dangerous or violent.

Stigmas affect a large percentage of people throughout the world. Some of the more common stigmas are associated with physical disabilities, mental health conditions, age, body type, gender, sexual orientation, nationality, family, ethnicity, race, religion, financial status, social sub-cultures and conduct. Stigmas set people apart from society and produce feelings in them of shame and isolation. People who are stigmatized are often considered socially unacceptable and they suffer prejudice, rejection, avoidance and discrimination.

What Can Be Done?
Fear of judgment and ridicule about moodiness often compels individuals and their families to hide away from society rather than face criticism, shunning, labeling and stereotyping. Instead of seeking treatment, they struggle in silence. Let's discuss some ways you can combat the stereotypes and stigmas that are associated with moodiness.

- You and your loved ones have choices. You can decide who is to know about your moodiness and what to tell them. You need not feel ashamed or embarrassed.
- You are not alone. Remember that many other people are coping with a similar situation.
- Seek help and remember that the activities in this workbook and treatment from medical professionals can help you to have productive careers and live satisfying lives.
- Be proactive and surround yourself with supportive people – people you can trust. Social isolation is a negative side effect of the stigma linked to moodiness. Isolating yourself and discontinuing enjoyable activities will not help.

How Can This Section Help Me?
The *Managing Moods Workbook* is designed to help you deal more effectively with your moodiness, and this section is specifically designed to help you overcome the stigma attached to moodiness. Complete the activities that follow to feel better about yourself, feel content, and become more resilient in the face of stress in your life.

Managing Moods

Two Types of Mental Health Stigma

Mental health stigma can be divided into two types:

1. **SOCIAL STIGMA is characterized by prejudicial attitudes and discriminating behavior directed towards individuals with mental health problems.**
2. **PERCEIVED STIGMA is the internalizing by the people with mental health conditions of their understanding of discrimination.**

Name some incidents when you felt people were judging you, talking about you or discriminating against you because of your moodiness. Next to your description of the incident, mark a number 1 or number 2, to indicate whether it was a social stigma or a perceived stigma. If you're not sure which, mark it with a question mark.

_____
_____
_____
_____
_____
_____
_____
_____
_____
_____
_____
_____
_____
_____
_____
_____
_____
_____

Often one perceives others' stigmatizing, or exaggerates others' or their own reactions.

The Stigma of Being Known as "Moody" – THE PAST

Mental health conditions can strike anyone! Mental conditions know no limits. During the course of a year, one or more mental health **conditions** such as moodiness will affect millions and millions of people.

Often the stigma attached to a mental health **condition** stops one from moving forward – being unable to talk about it for fear of being judged or labeled. We can erase the stigma of any mental health **conditions** by starting to discuss it with one person at a time, and taking the time to explain thoughts and feelings. Let's start with those people with whom you have already shared information about your moodiness.

With Whom Have You Discussed Your Moody Behaviors?	What Did You Say?	What Was This Person's Reaction? What Did the Person Say?	How Did You Feel?
Family			
Friends			
Acquaintances			
Co-workers			
Mental Health Professionals			

If any one of the above reacted in a negative way, to what do you attribute that reaction?

_____

_____

Managing Moods

The Stigma of Being Known as "Moody" – THE PRESENT

People often have perceptions about people who have mental health **conditions** and are moody. One of the ways to erase this stigma is to talk about it and let others know that people who are moody are just like anyone else who have some type of a condition.

Perhaps it is time to talk with other people whom you trust and/or with whom you feel safe.

Person with whom you might discuss your moody behaviors?	What would you say to this person?	What do you think this person's reaction might be?	What could you gain or lose by discussing it with this person?
Family			
Friends			
Acquaintances			
Co-workers			
Mental Health Professionals			
Others			

What Animal are YOU?

> *Animals don't lie. Animals don't criticize. If animals have moody days, they handle them better than humans do.*
> ~ *Betty White*

When you are in a moody frame of mind, what animal do you resemble?
_____

How do you resemble that animal? _____
_____
_____

How do people react to this animal-like behavior? _____
_____
_____

When you are NOT in a moody frame of mind, what animal do you resemble?
_____

How do you resemble that animal? _____
_____
_____

How do people react to this animal-like behavior? _____
_____
_____

Which animal do you like better and why? _____
_____
_____
_____

If we stamp out the stigma ...

Journal your thoughts about the following quotation:

If we stamp out the stigma attached to mental health issues, shed the shame and eliminate the fear, then we open the door for people to speak freely about what they are feeling and thinking. Then we enable individuals to seek help, get treatment and, hopefully, overcome their issue before it becomes extreme, scary and deadly.

~ Jaletta Albright Desmond

Erasing the Stigma of Mental Health Issues

My Trusted Social Network

It is important that you develop and maintain a network of people whom you can trust and in whom you can confide – people who do not stigmatize moodiness. These are the people who can make up your social network. They can be friends, family, co-workers, or people in your community – just about anyone. They are people with whom you feel, or might feel, comfortable discussing your roller coaster up and down emotions, and trust that they will help you manage your emotions without judging you. In the table below, list those people who are currently in your social network and those whom you would like to be in your social network.

People in My Current Social Network

Person	How I Know This Person	What I Can Tell This Person, Knowing I Will Not Be Judged

People I Would Like to Add to My Social Network

Person	How I Know This Person	How This Person Can Support Me

Managing Moods

Glenn Close said ...

*"The most powerful way to change someone's view is to meet them ...
People who do come out and talk about mental illness, that's when healing
can really begin. You can lead a productive life."*

Name a time when you have changed someone else's view – about anything. _____
_____
_____

How did that feel to you? _____
_____
_____

Name a time you were tempted to talk about your moodiness issue, but didn't? Why not? _____
_____
_____

Write about a situation in which you DID talk about your moodiness condition. _____
_____
_____

How did that feel? _____
How did it work out? _____
_____

Who is a trusted person you can talk with, to begin to heal? _____
Anyone else? _____
Who is a trusted person you can ask for a referral of someone to talk with, to begin to heal? _____
_____
Anyone else? _____
In an ideal world, how can you lead a more productive life? _____
_____
_____

How can you improve others' reactions to the stigma of moodiness, work on healing, and then create your ideal world? _____
_____
_____

Erasing the Stigma of Mental Health Issues

Effects of the Stigma of Moodiness

Check out these harmful effects of the stigma of being moody and write on the lines next to each item if it has affected you in some way and how.

1. Lack of understanding by family _____

2. Lack of understanding by friends _____

3. Lack of understanding by colleagues or others _____

4. Discrimination at work or school_____

5. Difficulty finding work or housing_____

6. Bullying, physical violence or harassment_____

7. Health insurance that doesn't adequately cover your issues _____

8. The belief that you will never be able to succeed or that you can't improve your situation._____

On the line of the corresponding number, write the name of a person you can speak to, a person who might help to support you about each of the situations you noted above. Add a reason you've chosen that person.

1. _____
2. _____
3. _____
4. _____
5. _____
6. _____
7. _____
8. _____

Managing Moods

Stereotypes

The social stigmas about moodiness often translate to the following inaccurate stereotypes. In the table below, write about how you are unlike the stereotype provided.

Stereotype	How I Defy That Stereotype
People who are moody lack willpower.	
Moody people's emotions are always out of control.	
People who are moody are dangerous to themselves or others.	
Moody people are just whiney and make excuses.	
People who are moody are antisocial.	
Other stereotypes of moody people.	

What would you like to say to other people who label you with these or other stereotypes?

_____

_____

Erasing the Stigma of Mental Health Issues

Coping with the Stigma of Moodiness

The stigma of having an condition such as moodiness is often more damaging than the moodiness itself. Athough we have come a long way, the acceptance of mental conditions is still a long way off. Learning to cope with your moodiness and the stigma that surrounds it will be helpful.

People treat you a bit differently. They might think of you as fragile, not knowing what your mood might be like, and they might avoid you altogether. What can you do about that? Consider educating them about your moodiness. What could you say?

_____
_____
_____

Use your own discretion. It is important for you and your well-being to be educated about your mood issue and to decide on whether to share and/or educate others. Trust your instinct. Educate and share with others with whom you are most comfortable. With whom are you comfortable telling about it and why?

_____
_____

With whom are you not comfortable telling about it and why?

_____
_____

Own your moodiness. Learn how to cope with it, dispel it and learn about it. What do you already know about it?

_____
_____
_____

Accept that you are special, worthwhile and have much to offer the world. Many famous people had the same condition (example Winston Churchill and Beethoven). What famous contemporary people have you read or heard about, who have mood conditions?

_____
_____
_____

Despite your moodiness, what is special about you and what do you have to offer to the world?

_____
_____

Managing Moods

What Can YOU Do?

"We have to get the word out that mental illnesses can be diagnosed and treated, and almost everyone suffering from mental illness can live meaningful lives in their communities."

~ Rosalynn Carter

How can YOU get the word out to erase the stigma of mental illness?

_____
_____
_____
_____
_____
_____
_____
_____
_____
_____

Brainstorm with a few other people how your group can get the word out to erase the stigma of mental illness?

_____
_____
_____
_____
_____
_____
_____
_____
_____
_____

Erasing the Stigma of Mental Health Issues

Focus on Your Strengths

You can do many things to help fight the stigma associated with moodiness. You can focus on your strengths rather than your limitations. Demonstrate to others that you have a great deal to offer. In the spaces that follow, identify some of your strengths. You have much to share, so take a few minutes to think about and write about some of your greatest strengths.

My strengths related to working:

_____
_____
_____

My strengths related to relationships with others:

_____
_____
_____

My strengths related to education and training:

_____
_____
_____

My strengths related to creativity:

_____
_____
_____

My strengths related to special skills I possess:

_____
_____
_____

How can you share these strengths to show others that even though you may be moody, you are still a capable, talented human being?

_____
_____
_____

Managing Moods

My Negative Thoughts

You can overcome the stigma of moodiness by refusing to worry about what others think. When you are worried about what others say about you, or might say about you, you might have constant thoughts that stop you from enjoying life. What are the negative thoughts that go through your head about others and what they think of you?

Others think I am ...

_____
_____
_____

Others don't think I can ...

_____
_____
_____

Others probably find me ...

_____
_____
_____

I think others might be afraid or wary of me because ...

_____
_____
_____

Others label me as ...

_____
_____
_____

Now that you have written these thoughts, take a big heavy black marker and put a big **X** through all of the thoughts above. When these negative thoughts come into your head, picture that big X, reminding you not to worry about what others think.

Erasing the Stigma of Mental Health Issues

Ways I Try to Minimize My Moodiness

Many people who are dealing with moodiness will try a variety of ways to minimize the negative affect that the stigma of moodiness has on them. Complete the following table to explore the various ways that you minimize your moodiness, how this makes you feel, and describe some better ways to cope.

Ways I Minimize My Moodiness	The Affect This Has on Me and Others	A Better Way to Cope
Example: I pretend that nothing is wrong with me. I scream at someone and then pretend that I am behaving fine.	*I feel sad and ashamed. People think I'm rude and don't want to be around me.*	*Explain that I get moody at times and I'm working on it.*
I pretend that nothing is wrong with me		
I refuse to get help		
I say things like "Nothing can ever help me"		
I will not to talk about my issues		
I laugh and make jokes about my behavior		
I avoid people		
Other		
Other		

Managing Moods

Ways I am Treated

Think about some of the ways that people treat you because of your moodiness. In the spaces below, explore the various ways people treat you. Write about those who treat you unfairly and why.

I am rejected by family:
(*Example: When I try to give my family input during discussion, they ignore me.*)

I am rejected by my friends.

I encounter problems at work.

I encounter problems at home.

I am subjected to physical violence or harassment.

I am laughed at.

I (you fill in the blank) _____

Erasing the Stigma of Mental Health Issues

Stay Active

Hiding away from other people because of your moodiness will not help you, nor will it show other people that moody people need support and understanding. It is important to remain active and continue engaging in activities that you enjoy. In the table below, identify some of the activities you enjoy, but have stopped engaging in and why.

Activity	Why I Stopped Doing It	How This Affected Me	What I Can Do in the Future
Example: Going to the gym	*People laughed when I became frustrated and kicked the bike.*	*I stopped going. Now I am sorry.*	*I can try to curb my frustration and if I do lash out, explain that I'm having mood issues and I'm working on it.*

Managing Moods

Self-Doubt

Don't let stigma create self-doubt and shame. One of the most important ways to minimize the stigma of moodiness is to explore how it makes you doubt yourself. Self-doubt almost always stems from a lack of understanding rather than information based on the facts. Feeling ashamed, embarrassed or humiliated because of something beyond your control can be very destructive. How does your moodiness cause you to doubt yourself and how can you control your self-doubt in a positive and strong way?

Ways I Doubt Myself	How This Negatively Affects Me	What I Can Do About it
Example: At a meeting I do not voice my opinion for fear of sounding angry or stupid.	I sit and say nothing and I think people wonder why I'm there.	I choose my words carefully. I make sure I'm saying something positive as well as whatever I need to say.

However you arrive at the ability to ignore self-doubt – if you can acquire it or possess it or find it or discover it – move beyond self-doubt.

~ Dwight Yoakum

How do you relate to this_____
_____

Erasing the Stigma of Mental Health Issues

A Poster About the Stigma of Moodiness

In the space that follows, draw a picture of how you believe moodiness looks in people when they are stigmatized by others.

Managing Moods

DE-STIGMA-TIZE with the Facts About Mental Health Issues

Myth: Mental health issues are rare.
  Fact: Mental health issues are not rare and affect nearly everyone either directly or indirectly.

Myth: People with mental health issues are unable to lead productive lives.
  Fact: Most people with a mental health issue respond to treatment, learn to cope with and manage their problems, and go on to lead productive and fulfilling lives.

Myth: People who have mental health issues will not get better.
  Fact: Once diagnosed, mental health issues are treatable. While they are not always cured, they can be managed effectively. Most people with mental health conditions live productive and positive lives while receiving treatments for their mental health issue. As is the case with any illness, individuals with severe or persistent mental health conditions who respond poorly to available treatments may require more support and may not function as highly as others.

Myth: People with serious mental health issues are violent and unpredictable.
  Fact: While some people who suffer from serious mental health issues do commit antisocial acts, mental health issues do not equal criminality or violence – despite the media's tendency to emphasize a suspected link. People with mental health issues are no more likely to commit violence than any one in the general public, but they are more likely to be victimized and are more likely to inflict violent behaviors on themselves.

Myth: Mental health issues happen because of bad parenting or personal weakness.
  Fact: The main risk factors for mental health issues are not bad parenting or personal weakness but rather genetics, severe and prolonged stress (such as physical or sexual abuse), or other environmental influences (such as birth trauma or head injury).

Myth: Treatments for mental health issues are not usually effective.
  Fact: The effectiveness of any treatment depends on a number of factors including the type of mental health issue and the particular needs of the individual. A combination of psychiatric medication and psychotherapy, or social interventions are the most effective way to treat mental health issues.

Myth: Mental health conditions are caused by everyday stressors.
  Fact: It may seem that stress is responsible for mental health conditions; however, there is no one clear cause of mental health conditions. Rather, it is a result of complex interactions between psychological, biological, genetic and social factors. Stress, stigma, and lack of support can make it worse on the individual.

Myth: Mental health issues are always hereditary.
  Fact: Some mental health issues include a genetic component, which results in a predisposition or vulnerability toward the mental health problems among children and siblings, but environment also plays a key role in the development of certain conditions. If someone in one's family has a mental health condition, that person will be at higher risk.

If you start to experience the symptoms of a mental health condition, it is important for you to see a mental health professional to determine if you have a problem that will require treatment. If you know of anyone who seems to have symptoms of a mental health condition, urge them to do the same.

wholeperson

Whole Person Associates is the leading publisher of training resources for professionals who empower people to create and maintain healthy lifestyles. Our creative resources will help you work effectively with your clients in the areas of stress management, wellness promotion, mental health and life skills.

Please visit us at our web site: **www.wholeperson.com**. You can check out our entire line of products, place an order, request our print catalog, and sign up for our monthly special notifications.

Whole Person Associates

800-247-6789